GREAT FILMMAKERS
STEVEN SPIELBERG

Wil Mara

Cavendish Square

New York

Published in 2015 by Cavendish Square Publishing, LLC
243 5th Avenue, Suite 136, New York, NY 10016

Library of Congress Cataloging-in-Publication Data

Mara, Wil.
 Steven Spielberg / Wil Mara.
   pages cm. — (Great filmmakers)
 Includes index.
 ISBN 978-1-62712-936-7 (hardcover) ISBN 978-1-62712-938-1 (ebook)
 1. Spielberg, Steven, 1946—-Juvenile literature. 2. Motion picture producers and directors—United
States—Biography—Juvenile literature. I. Title.

 PN1998.3.S65M273 2014
 791.43'0233'092—dc23
 [B]

                         2013050651

Editorial Director: Dean Miller   Designer: Amy Greenan
Editor: Fletcher Doyle   Production Manager: Jennifer Ryder-Talbot
Senior Copy Editor: Wendy A. Reynolds   Production Editor: David McNamara
Art Director: Jeffrey Talbot   Photo Researcher: J8 Media

GREAT FILMMAKERS
STEVEN SPIELBERG

1 THE STORY BEGINS

A Most Remarkable Personality

Steven Allan Spielberg came into the world shortly after 6:00 PM on December 18, 1946, in Cincinnati, Ohio. His father, Arnold, was an electrical engineer of Russian descent, and his mother, Leahanni, was a restaurateur and concert pianist whose family emigrated from Poland to the United States. Steven's parents would go on to have three more children in the years ahead, all girls—Anne, Susan, and Nancy.

As the firstborn child, young Steven received a great amount of adoration from his relatives. He enjoyed this positive attention very much, and his desire for more would become one of the driving factors in his life. His tireless curiosity while growing up is also noteworthy. Spielberg never accepted anything at face value, and would wear down friends and family members with a seemingly

Spielberg in the mid 1970s, already well on his way to unimaginable success.

endless litany of questions, as if he had an inborn fear of the unknown. He was the type of child who would take something apart to find out how it worked, or look under a bed or behind a door just to see what was hidden from view.

Spielberg's inquisitive nature was paired with another remarkable quality—energy. While most children are viewed as being energetic, Spielberg was on another level. When he became involved in a project, he would work on it to the exclusion of everything else, including everyday tasks such as eating. Nevertheless, many adults were quietly impressed by the seriousness and deep focus he devoted to his interests at such an early age.

One of the personality traits Spielberg exhibited early on that did not endear him to many people was a mischievousness that could sometimes be thoughtless and harsh. He was particularly fond of destroying things as a child, and had little regard for other people's property or hard work. According to Spielberg biographer Joseph McBride in his 2010 book, *Steven Spielberg: A Biography*, Spielberg once threw a pie his mother had baked onto the ceiling, just so he could watch it ooze back down. He and some friends also smashed windows in a newly constructed building, which resulted in tens of thousands of dollars' worth of damage. He often picked on his younger sisters, and took great delight in using his prodigious imagination to scare them half to death.

Spielberg's personality was a blend of traits from his mother and father. His father possessed tremendous intelligence and, like his son, he could not accept things simply as they were—he always had to know more. Arnold Spielberg was also admired for his dogged perseverance and capacity for hard work. Steven's mother, on the other hand, was a much more liberal and free-spirited personality. Leahanni wasn't afraid to think differently from the rest of society, and had a strong independent streak. She was a naturally positive and open-minded individual with an even temper and a love of all things artistic. Steven inherited her willingness to step outside of convention and follow her own path, as well as her love for all forms of art and creativity.

Jewish in a World of Gentiles

Although World War II had ended in 1945, it was still fresh on most people's minds in America when Spielberg was born—the Jewish-Americans in particular. During the war, Jews were targeted by Adolf Hitler and his murderous program of "ethnic cleansing" in Europe. During this period, also known as the **Holocaust**, Hitler's Nazi Party oversaw the death of literally millions of Jews. The Spielbergs were Orthodox Jews, and some of young Steven's relatives and family friends had survived the Holocaust. The stories he heard as a child of their suffering chilled him.

Spielberg's family left their predominantly Jewish neighborhood in Ohio in the early 1950s and moved around the country for his father's different work assignments—first to New Jersey, then Arizona, and finally to California. Over the years, they lived in a few neighborhoods that were populated mostly by **Gentiles**—a term for non-Jewish people—some of whom were not friendly toward Jews. Spielberg and his family often faced a dislike of Jews called **anti-Semitism**, which is similar to the bigotry aimed at other religions and ethnicities.

Some families refused to let their children play with Steven, and he was sometimes bullied for being Jewish. In a *New York Times* article in 1993, Spielberg admitted, "I was embarrassed, I was self-conscious, I was always aware I stood out because of my Jewishness. In high school, I got smacked and kicked around. Two bloody noses. It was horrible." This self-consciousness led to Spielberg becoming more socially withdrawn as the years went by, particularly when he started school.

School Struggles

Spielberg often felt like an outsider at school. He was not particularly athletic, and he never felt welcome among any of the "popular" kids. He made a few friends, most of whom felt as out of place as he did, but also kept to himself a lot of the time. This did not mean he spent more time studying, however.

His parents were uncommonly intelligent, and as he was obviously very bright and inquisitive, Spielberg was expected from a young age to do well academically. In truth, he was an average student for most of his school years and was often accused by teachers and school administrators of being indifferent and inattentive. He would do only the minimum amount of schoolwork needed to get by and no more, and often waited to finish his homework and other assignments until the last minute. Even his mother, who was always supportive of him, expressed disappointment at what she considered his lazy attitude toward schoolwork.

Unbeknownst to the entire family, Spielberg had **dyslexia**—a reading disability that prevents the brain from recognizing and processing certain letters and symbols in the correct order—which contributed to his academic struggles and led to a lot of his frustration at school. Dyslexia is treatable, but Steven Spielberg was not diagnosed until he was 60 years old. In a 2012 interview, Spielberg said that his diagnosis with dyslexia was "like the last puzzle part in a tremendous mystery that I've kept to myself all these years... Dyslexia led me to realize that I was different." He admits that he still struggles with reading. "Even today it still takes me longer to read a movie **script** or a book than anyone else... It takes me two hours and 45 minutes to read what others can read in one hour and 10 minutes." However, he never let his undiagnosed reading problem stop him from reaching his goals.

As Spielberg grew older, he began to slip further into a creative world of his own making that took up most of his time, energy, and concentration. Even while attending Hebrew school a few afternoons a week—where he would study the finer points of Judaism—Spielberg often detached himself from the center of activity.

A Lonely Boy Finds a World to Call Home

Most loners begin to blossom when they discover a world where they fit in, and it was no different with young Steven. He took his first step toward discovering such a world while the family was living in Camden, New Jersey in 1952, when his father took him to see his first movie. Called *The Greatest Show on Earth*, the film was set in the Ringling Brothers and Barnum & Bailey Circus and boasted some of the biggest stars of the day, including Jimmy Stewart,

The Greatest Show on Earth, a film that Spielberg saw as a child, sparked a fascination with cinema that never left him.

Dorothy Lamour, and Charlton Heston. Combining a fast-paced plot with behind-the-scenes circus footage, *The Greatest Show on Earth* went on to win the 1952 **Academy Award** for Best Picture. In spite of all this, six-year-old Steven was at first annoyed to be sitting in the darkened movie theater—he had misunderstood his father and thought they were going to an *actual* circus.

Despite his initial disappointment, the way that a story could be told on a large, flat screen in full color left a deep impression on him and fueled his creativity. In his 50-Year History of International Achievement Summit address in 2006, Spielberg remembered it as a turning point in his young life, saying, "I was no longer in a theater. I was no longer in a seat, or aware of the surroundings…I became part of the experience." As he grew into adolescence, his appreciation for storytelling grew along with him, and soon he was in possession of a very fertile imagination.

Steven's father has been a source of great stories to draw from during his filmmaking career. His father's long working hours meant frequent absences from home, which often left the small boy feeling betrayed—but he cherished his father's habit of tucking him into bed on the evenings he was home. Arnold could often be as creative as Steven's mother, and would make up fantastic stories for his son's amusement. Other times, he would hold his son spellbound with stories of his own World War II experiences, as well as those of his friends.

Spielberg also found inspiration in the medium of television. In the 1950s, many homes did not have a TV set. However, because Arnold worked in the electronics industry, the Spielbergs owned one.

Steven was fascinated by the possibility of telling great stories and then being able to deliver them to a little box that sat in someone's living room. He became so entranced by the TV in his own home that his parents had to limit the number of hours he was allowed to watch, lest his schoolwork suffer even further. Soon, Spielberg was making up stories of his own, and acting them out with neighborhood friends using household items as props.

Junior Filmmaker

Another major moment in the making of Steven Spielberg came in 1952. Shortly after the family moved to Arizona, Steven's father received an eight-millimeter movie camera as a gift from his wife. Arnold used it primarily to film family trips and other outings, and it wasn't long before Steven was criticizing the quality of his productions. Frustrated, Arnold suggested that Steven take over all family filming duties—and Steven enthusiastically agreed. Ironically, now it was Arnold's turn to complain about the unusual camera techniques Steven experimented with while documenting their family life, but Steven didn't care that much—he enjoyed having the power to choose what to film, how best to shoot it, and how to make an everyday event in his family's life tell a bigger story.

It was around this time that Steven Spielberg made his first "feature" film. Inspired by a scene from *The Greatest Show on Earth*, he painstakingly set up and filmed two of his toy trains crashing into each other. Pleased with his success, he was soon walking around the neighborhood filming everything that struck him as interesting.

As soon as Spielberg got his hands on his
first eight-millimeter camera, he began
shooting movies.

This came with a fringe benefit Spielberg had not
expected—many of the neighborhood kids wanted
to be in his films, and suddenly they were treating
him very differently than before. He soon became
the center of attention, and was fairly popular.
This also gave him a confidence that he hadn't
previously possessed. A handful of kids even joined
him, borrowing their own parents' cameras and
making little films. It is interesting to note that the
suburban settings seen in many of Spielberg's most
famous movies bear a strong resemblance to those
he filmed for the shorts he made as a kid walking
around his Arizona neighborhood.

As Spielberg's interest in filmmaking continued to
grow, so did his need to buy more film. His parents
bankrolled him up to a point, but they also wanted
him to learn something about the value of money. To
earn the extra cash he needed, Spielberg came up

A MERITORIOUS EFFORT

Young Steven was a member of the Boy Scouts of America, and one of the first movies he ever directed was made in an attempt to earn the rank of Eagle Scout. His father suggested that he try for a merit badge in the photography category by making a short film. Spielberg wrote a storyline about a Western-style shootout and called it *The Last Gunfight*. While his father did most of the actual filming and his friends were the actors, everything in the production was done under Steven's careful guidance and direction. When he showed the finished film to his scout troop, they were delighted, and Spielberg earned his badge. *The Last Gunfight* was clearly a sign of things to come.

with the idea of showing his films, as well as any popular movies of the day that he could get copies of, to friends and neighbors at his parents' house. Using the copy machine in his father's office, he made posters and hung them around town. He also had his sisters run a concession stand where refreshments were sold during intermissions. The films were often shown on a large white bed sheet hung from a clothesline in the Spielbergs' backyard. After the movies ended, Spielberg would ask the audience questions about the things they did and didn't like. His knowledge of what people wanted to see grew, and he ventured into different movie **genres**, including Westerns, horror, war dramas, local documentaries, and slapstick comedies to meet the demand.

A Course is Set

By the time Spielberg began attending Phoenix's Arcadia High School in 1961, filmmaking was an all-consuming passion. While most fourteen-year-old kids were interested in cars, sports, dating, and generally goofing off, Spielberg was becoming ever more serious about what he saw as a possible profession. He once again found himself set apart from the majority of his classmates, and since he was now just one person among a student body of thousands, he withdrew even further into his own world. He frequently got into trouble for cutting classes or skipping entire school days so he could work on his latest project. When he did show up, his attention usually didn't arrive with him.

His father was particularly disappointed about his poor academic performance, as he had always

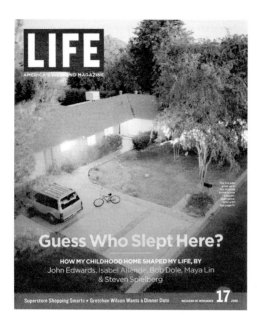

This cover of *Life* magazine shows the house where Spielberg lived as a teen, in the Arcadia neighborhood that straddled Scottsdale and Phoenix, Arizona (opposite).

hoped that Steven would focus on becoming an engineer or perhaps even a physician. Still struggling with his undiagnosed dyslexia, Spielberg tried his best in school. However, he was extremely frustrated in his classes, and these careers required a greater dedication to learning math and science than he was willing to give. Steven didn't even want to sacrifice his time on romance—he rarely dated, and those girls who fell for him were usually soon frustrated by his lack of interest. In spite of all the disappointment that swirled around him, filmmaking was far more than just a hobby, and he pursued it relentlessly. Young Steven had a dream, and he had every intention of seeing it come true.

2 GETTING BETTER ALL THE TIME

From Amateur to Young Pro

In 1961, fourteen-year-old Spielberg made a short World War II film called *Escape to Nowhere*. It was shot on eight-millimeter film in full color, but with no sound. *Escape to Nowhere* follows American soldiers trying to take a hill in Africa while surrounded by Germans. Spielberg used friends and family members as actors and shot most of the footage in the Arizona desert. In spite of these constraints, the film was very realistic and evocative, and it won first place in an Arizona amateur film contest. His prize included some much-needed film equipment. Steven's father, who had helped with *Escape to Nowhere* and was impressed by the results, also bought his son the equipment required to shoot with sound. Armed with these upgraded tools, Spielberg was ready to take the next step.

Spielberg on the **set** of 1974's *The Sugarland Express,* the first feature film he directed for Universal.

That step would be *Firelight*, a film he made in 1964 about a group of people investigating what appears to be the abduction of citizens by aliens in a small Arizona town. Seventeen-year-old Spielberg wrote the screenplay, built the props, created (along with his father) some realistic special effects, and even wrote the musical **score**. Much of the shooting was done on the weekends to accommodate Spielberg's school schedule, and often at night to avoid the desert heat. Although he was still so young, his maturity on the set was remarkable. Many of the actors remember him being calm and respectful, and able to obtain the best performances from everyone. Whenever problems arose during the production, he would handle them with remarkable confidence. In turn, the cast and crew wanted to do their best for him.

Hollywood at Last

Shortly after *Firelight* was completed, the Spielbergs moved to California. At this point, Steven was a junior in high school — and Arnold and Leahanni's marriage was on the rocks. Their parents' constant arguing had a powerful effect on all the Spielberg children, and Steven responded by diving even deeper into his filmmaking.

In the summer of 1964, he worked part time as an unpaid intern at **Universal Studios** in Hollywood. This was the first step into the world of his dreams. Chuck Silvers, who was the head of Universal's film library, was impressed by Spielberg from the start, and admired the teenager's focus, energy, curiosity, and ambition. He also thought *Firelight* was an excellent piece of work, particularly given the limited

Universal Studios added to its facilities in 1963 with a project that included thirty-one sound stages. Universal would be Spielberg's professional home for many years.

equipment and money Spielberg had at his disposal. Silvers would go on to become a mentor to the budding filmmaker.

In truth, Spielberg's early days at Universal were fairly boring. He was given small tasks like handling paperwork, answering phones, and sorting through mail. However, he also had access to every sector of the film industry. Spielberg wandered the lots during the day and watched filming in progress. Soon he became friendly with people on every level of the business, and most were happy to answer his questions. By studying the way the professionals interacted, he learned what it took to make a major motion picture.

Not everything was going as smoothly for Spielberg during this period. At home, the tension

THE TIMES WERE A-CHANGIN'

By the late 1960s, many young talents had begun to break onto the filmmaking scene, including future heavyweights such as Francis Ford Coppola, Martin Scorsese, and Spielberg's future good friend, George Lucas (at left in the photo). These filmmakers were interested in experimentation and new ideas, and, along with Steven, would usher in a new age as the Hollywood studio system collapsed. This collapse, led in large part by the death of former studio mogul Louis B. Mayer in 1957 and Darryl F. Zanuck's permanent retirement as the head of 20th Century Fox in 1971, was a testament to the increasing draw of television, which now competed with movies for audiences. Spielberg and the other new filmmakers were the first generation to grow up watching television, and were heavily influenced by the way the medium often combined compelling, sometimes intimate stories with special effects for greater impact.

between his parents was worsening. When his father accepted a very good job at IBM, the family moved to Saratoga, California, an area near San Jose with very few Jewish people, and they again experienced anti-Semitism. With his father at work most of the time, and his mother and sisters miserable and desperate to move back to Arizona, Steven was left feeling lonely and conflicted.

Spielberg has said that he also suffered in school during this period. Thanks to his filmmaking successes and his Universal Studios internship, he was much more advanced than kids his own age. It was hard for him to forge meaningful relationships with classmates he had so little in common with. He often became depressed and frustrated when he wasn't at Universal, where he felt understood and accepted. As a result of these personal hardships, he withdrew further into himself. Still struggling with his undiagnosed dyslexia, Spielberg found it even harder to concentrate, and his schoolwork suffered. Even today, Spielberg considers it one of the worst times of his life. Looking back on it in an interview with the *Examiner* in September of 2012, Spielberg said, "Movies really helped me... kind of saved me from shame, from guilt... Making movies was my great escape."

Breaking Through

Spielberg graduated from Saratoga High School in 1965. His parents divorced, agreeing that Leahanni and the girls would go back to Arizona, while Steven and his father moved to Los Angeles, keeping Steven close to the film industry. Poor grades kept him out of the prestigious film school at the

University of Southern California, so he enrolled in California State University at Long Beach, which offered basic courses in television and filmmaking.

This was a transitional period for both Spielberg and the industry he loved, and he recognized the value of it. He continued hanging around Universal in his spare time, making connections with actors, **directors**, **editors**, cameramen, and other behind-the-scenes professionals. He would get thrown off a set every once in a while, but his persistence and sheer ambition always led him back. He just wouldn't quit. One way or another, he was going to become a professional filmmaker, and he knew the window of opportunity would not stay open forever.

In 1967, while still an intern at Universal, he began making a new film about bicycle racing called *Slipstream*. He'd raised $5,000 for the movie's budget, believing that would be enough. However, Spielberg ran out of money before *Slipstream* could be completed. Undaunted, he set about on his next project—one that would change his life.

Amblin' Toward a Career

Amblin', a 26-minute short film, is a love story set in the late '60s. It's about a boy and girl who come together while hitchhiking to the beaches of California, and who end the relationship once they reach their destination. Spielberg didn't enjoy the free-spirited, hippie-like feel of the story, but he did find people who would put up the money to make it. He also realized that the film would appeal to certain movie fans.

This time, the young director had scraped together $20,000—the minimum needed. Spielberg, now an expert at cutting corners and creating inventive solutions to problems, made the most of the opportunity. While he was not paid for his work on the film, he did get full credit as writer and director, which furthered his career—and that was what he really wanted.

Spielberg impressed everyone with his beyond-his-years wisdom and professionalism. He could be demanding on the set, but there were no doubts among his crew that his greatest interest was in telling the best story possible. When shooting was done, he spent weeks editing the footage, sitting in a cutting room seven days a week. *Amblin'* was released in December 1968 and was regarded as a success by both critics and moviegoers. It also won multiple awards, and was featured at the prestigious Atlantic Film Festival the following year.

Sidney Sheinberg was instrumental in helping Spielberg get his start as a director.

More importantly, *Amblin'* caught the attention of a very powerful figure at Universal, and Spielberg's short film proved to be the key to opening the door to his success.

A Career Begins

Sidney Sheinberg was the vice president of Universal's television production division. A lawyer skilled at negotiating, Sheinberg was a no-nonsense executive known for making decisions designed to move things forward. He predicted many of the changes coming to the film and television industry, and felt certain that young Spielberg was going to play a major part in those changes. He realized that it would be better for Spielberg to work for Universal instead of a competitor. In 1968, Sheinberg signed him to a seven-year contract, and Spielberg dropped out of college and became the youngest director ever to be signed for a long-term deal with a major Hollywood studio.

Spielberg was just twenty-one, and he was thrilled. For his parents, it was a bittersweet moment—while they were happy that he was advancing in a profession he clearly loved, they weren't delighted that he quit college just a year short of a degree. He never forgot this, and, in 2002, Spielberg—one of the world's most famous filmmakers—returned to California State University at Long Beach and finished his bachelor's degree in film and electronic arts at the age of fifty-five. Addressing the graduating class in his cap and gown, he said, "I wanted to accomplish this for many years as a 'thank you' to my parents for giving me the opportunity for an education and a career, and as a personal note for my own family—and young people everywhere—about the importance of achieving their college education goals."

The day after Spielberg left college in 1968, he began work on his first Universal television project— an episode of the popular show *Night Gallery*. The brainchild of legendary writer Rod Serling (who also created the iconic series *The Twilight Zone*), *Night Gallery* featured a weekly story from the world of the dark and macabre. Spielberg would be responsible for one of the pilot episodes starring Academy Award-winning actress Joan Crawford. The idea of working with Crawford made Spielberg terribly nervous. He was also concerned because he felt the script was poorly written. However, he knew he'd been given an amazing opportunity, and he worked hard to make the best of it.

Crawford took an instant liking to him, particularly because he had reached a position of such importance through sheer hard work and determination. Crawford had clawed her way to the top at a young age in a similar manner, and was very impressed

Joan Crawford was one of the first major stars Spielberg directed. They became friends.

with her young director. While Spielberg found the experience exhausting and sometimes frustrating, he learned a great deal and, most importantly, established himself as a capable director who could see a job through to completion. While the episode ended up getting so-so reviews from critics, it earned excellent viewer ratings, and he and Crawford remained friends until her death in 1977.

Spielberg worked on other TV projects for Universal while patiently waiting for the chance to do what he really wanted—a feature film. He directed a TV movie in 1971 called *LA 2017*, which is set in a futuristic Los Angeles among a terrified population controlled by a government of psychiatrists. *LA 2017* was part of an NBC series called *The Name of the*

Game, and he did a fine job with it. However, it was his next TV movie opportunity that would really catch the public's attention.

Duel was based on a story by writer Richard Matheson, who had also been responsible for many of *The Twilight Zone* scripts. *Duel* is a disturbing tale of an ordinary man in a small car being stalked by the unseen, nameless driver of a huge tanker truck on an otherwise lonely desert highway. Spielberg shot the film along the roadways of California and completed it in less than two weeks. It was released in November of 1971 as part of ABC's *Movie of the Week* series. The American public's response was so overwhelmingly positive that Universal decided to offer it on television in other countries as well. *Duel* was such a huge hit with international viewers that Universal had Spielberg go back and shoot some additional scenes in order to make the film longer, and released it as a feature film in theaters around the United States. Public and critical reaction to the longer version was excellent, enhancing Spielberg's fast-growing reputation. Universal Studios' executives decided it was time for Spielberg to graduate from TV and make a feature film specifically for theater audiences.

Jaws

Spielberg's first feature film intended for theaters was released in 1974. Called *The Sugarland Express*, the plot revolves around a woman who helps her convict husband break out of prison because they are at risk of losing their son to a foster home. While *The Sugarland Express* told an interesting story, and critics thought Spielberg did a respectable job of

Spielberg joined his crew in the surf while filming *Jaws*—his first blockbuster.

directing it, it did not find a large audience and made only a modest profit in theaters.

Spielberg shook off this setback and dived right into his next film, which would take a big step toward making him a household name. Writer Peter Benchley had scored a tremendous success with *Jaws*, a novel about the hunt for a great white shark that terrorizes beachgoers in a small resort town. For Spielberg, turning Benchley's novel into a movie was a golden opportunity to tell the kind of tale he once used to terrify his younger sisters. He signed on as director in June of 1973, and received a budget of about $3.5 million and a shooting schedule of just under two months.

Spielberg had no trouble complying with budget and schedule limitations on his previous projects,

Jaws became a hit in large part because it made a familiar place, the beach, a frightening **location**.

but he could not have foreseen all the problems awaiting him with *Jaws*. First, Spielberg kept requesting adjustments to the script, which was rewritten several times by various **screenwriters**. The casting process became unusually arduous: the studio wanted big-name actors, whereas Spielberg felt that using celebrities for the cast would be too distracting. In his mind, the shark should be the real star of the film.

Then, during production, there were endless problems with the mechanical sharks. This was an age well before **computer-generated imagery (CGI)**, so the fake sharks had to look and behave in a believable manner on camera. The sharks, however, kept malfunctioning or breaking down, which caused delays in filming, Also, some of the actors experienced seasickness on the set, so scenes had to be shot multiple times, driving the film way over budget. The movie ultimately surpassed its schedule by more than one hundred days and went over budget by more than $5 million. Spielberg was convinced his career as a director was finished because of this.

He could not have been more mistaken.

Jaws hit theaters on June 20, 1975 and was an immediate smash. **Box office** ticket sales soared, and the movie recouped its production expenses in just two weeks. Less than three months later, it sailed past the most successful North American film up to that point (*The Godfather*), earning more than $100 million at the box office (the first film in North America ever to do so). It earned hundreds of millions more when it was released on video, both in the United States and abroad. *Jaws* would become the highest-grossing film of all time—a title it would hold until *Star Wars*, written and directed by Spielberg's close friend George Lucas, was released in 1977 and began its own epic run.

The once-awkward, inquisitive, and energetic little boy who made home movies in Arizona had become one of the most in-demand directors in the world. And while he might have considered the success of *Jaws* a dream come true, Spielberg had no way of knowing the dream had only just begun.

3 MR. BLOCKBUSTER

Out of This World

Spielberg had long wanted to do a big-budget science fiction film in the spirit of his amateur production, *Firelight*. Neither Universal Studios nor 20th Century Fox, another of the biggest studios in the world, was interested in the idea—but a third, Columbia Pictures, felt the project was worthwhile. In the latter half of 1973, while finishing work on *The Sugarland Express*, Spielberg signed a deal with Columbia and began developing the project.

Spielberg wanted the script to focus on human interaction with unidentified flying objects, or UFOs, and he worked with a few screenwriters. He did so much of the writing himself on the final version that he ended being the only writer who got screenwriting credit for it. Called *Close Encounters of the Third Kind*, the film follows one ordinary man, Roy Neary, who has what he feels to be a legitimate

This image from *Close Encounters of the Third Kind* has become one of the most iconic in film history.

UFO sighting. Many in Hollywood thought a film about UFOs was a guaranteed bomb, especially from a filmmaker with so little experience. However, Columbia had faith in Spielberg, which only increased after the success of *Jaws*. The studio gave him not only a budget of around $20 million, but also a free hand to shoot the movie.

Filming began in May of 1976, and, as with *Jaws*, Spielberg experienced numerous technical and financial problems. As a result, the film missed its intended release in the summer of 1977. This turned out to be a fortunate turn of events, as George Lucas had released the first of his massively successful *Star Wars* films at that time, and the two would have competed. Instead, *Close Encounters* was released in November 1977 and became Columbia Pictures' most successful movie ever. Nominated for eight Academy Awards, it, along with *Star Wars*, led to a renewed public interest in outer space movies. For Spielberg, it was a huge triumph—not only was he now a household name, he was also an established directorial star in Hollywood. After so many years of hard work, Spielberg had finally arrived.

Ups and Downs

The next few years would prove to be a roller coaster ride for Spielberg in terms of box-office success. Following the enormous success of *Close Encounters*, Spielberg set his sights on a relatively new genre for him—comedy. His next movie, entitled *1941*, is about a Los Angeles community's panicked reaction to the Japanese attacks on Pearl Harbor. The film is essentially a collection of short stories tied together by wartime paranoia, told with a large helping of humor. While it did fairly well at the box office, *1941* didn't come close to the success of *Close Encounters*.

After the lukewarm reaction to *1941*, there were people in the film industry who had doubts about Spielberg's ability to bounce back with a hit. They would be silenced by his next project: *Raiders of the Lost Ark*. Henry "Indiana" Jones, the hero of the film, was actually the creation of Spielberg's friend George Lucas. The two had been vacationing together in Hawaii in 1977, following the release of Lucas's first *Star Wars* installment (Lucas wanted to be out of town in case *Star Wars* flopped). During their vacation, Lucas shared with Spielberg his idea for a character who leads a dual life—half dusty old college professor, half daring adventurer. Spielberg loved the idea, and together they developed the storyline for *Raiders*. Indy's thrilling quest to find the Ark of the Covenant before Hitler's Nazis reach it made *Raiders* one of the biggest-grossing films of all time.

Raiders of the Lost Ark was a joint effort between the two men, but it was Spielberg who ended up in the director's chair. Filming began in June of 1980 with a budget of just under $20 million, and took Spielberg and his crew to various locations in the United States, England, France, and

Spielberg and his good friend George Lucas (left) made *Raiders of the Lost Ark* together.

HORRORS ON THE SCREEN— AND OFF

Anyone who thinks making movies is all glitz and glamor should think again. Although *Raiders of the Lost Ark* became a smash success, its production had some scary moments. The cast and crew had to interact with cobras, one of which spread its hood in front of lead actor Harrison Ford in what would become one of the most famous images in modern film history (although there was a pane of glass between them, so Ford was never in any actual danger). And, while shooting in Tunisia, everyone became ill from food poisoning—everyone, that is, except Spielberg, who'd had the foresight to bring along canned food.

Tunisia. *Raiders* hit theaters in June of 1981 and became one of the biggest hits of all time, earning more than $335 million at the box office. The character of Indiana Jones was so popular that the public soon demanded more. In time, Spielberg and Lucas would give it to them.

In 1981, Spielberg oversaw the launch of another dream project—his own film production company. He founded Amblin Entertainment (named after *Amblin'*, the 1968 short film that landed him his first studio contract) as a means of retaining a degree of creative independence outside of the movies he made with large studios like Universal. Spielberg would use Amblin to produce the films of other directors, and those films would be distributed and financed through other studios beyond Universal.

Out-Of-This-World Success With *E.T.*

Following the massive success of *Raiders*, Spielberg was soon deep in his next film, a touching story of unconventional friendship called *E.T. the Extra-Terrestrial*. In the film, E.T. is a gentle, wide-eyed creature from another planet that gets stranded on Earth. He is discovered by a little boy named Elliot, who lives in the American suburbs with his family. It doesn't take long for the government to get wind of the possibility that a being from another world has taken up temporary residence, and Elliot and his siblings do everything they can to keep E.T. safe until he is able to be reunited with his spaceship.

Spielberg and screenwriter Melissa Mathison put the story together, and Spielberg shot the film in the fall of 1981. When the finished product reached the public in June of 1982, it made movie history.

Produced on a budget of just over $10 million, *E.T.* went on to earn more than three-quarters of a billion dollars in ticket sales alone. It became the highest-earning film to that point and was hailed by critics and audiences as one of the greatest sci-fi films ever made. One image from the movie—that of Elliot "flying" his BMX bicycle across the night sky, with E.T. sitting on the handlebars and a giant moon behind them—has since become an icon of 1980s American culture. This image also became the logo for Spielberg's production company, Amblin Entertainment.

E.T. was the first of his five movies inducted into the **National Film Registry** by the Library of Congress' National Film Preservation Board. The National Film Preservation Board was created in 1988 to preserve films it deemed "culturally, historically or esthetically important." It selects twenty-five films each year to the registry. *E.T.* was inducted in 1994, and was followed by *Raiders of the Lost Ark* in 1999, *Jaws* in 2001, *Schindler's List* in 2004, and *Close Encounters of the Third Kind* in 2007.

Spielberg added to his success with a series of scary films. The first, *Poltergeist*, involves a suburban family of five whose youngest child, a daughter named Carol Anne, is abducted by ghosts and taken into another dimension. With equal parts terror and determination, Carol Anne's parents take the dangerous steps to get her back. Released just a week before *E.T.* and made with roughly the same budget, *Poltergeist* did not do as well but was still a massive success, so much so that some began referring to the summer of '82 as "the summer of Spielberg." Spielberg wrote and produced *Poltergeist* but was not directly involved in directing it (although there have been rumors suggesting he

This image from *E.T.*—another Spielberg blockbuster—has also become one of the most familiar and beloved in American culture.

contributed to the directorial effort in small ways). He later said that he particularly enjoyed the movie because it touched upon his love of scaring the wits out of people.

Sticking with this approach, he then directed "Kick the Can," one of four segments for the 1983 movie adaptation of *The Twilight Zone*, which had been enormously popular as a television program from 1959 to 1964. Spielberg also co-produced *The Twilight Zone* movie with fellow director John Landis, and while the film was not nearly as successful as either *E.T.* or *Poltergeist*, it still made a profit.

Although directing is his first love, Spielberg has also served as a **producer** on several projects. A producer is the top overseer of a film, and is responsible for everything from finding and developing the storylines to obtaining the necessary funding, as well as hiring directors, actors, and crew. On 1984's *Gremlins*, for example—a film about small and cute but highly destructive creatures called Mogwai—Spielberg acted as producer, but did not direct. Another blockbuster, *Gremlins* earned more than $150 million at the box office and inspired a wave of Mogwai-oriented merchandise.

Indiana Jones and the Temple of Doom

The first Indiana Jones movie, *Raiders of the Lost Ark*, had been such a huge success that Spielberg and Lucas felt compelled to make another. Rather than make a sequel, they decided instead to make a "prequel"—a movie whose plot is set before, rather than after, that of the first successful film. In the *Raiders* prequel, titled *Indiana Jones and the Temple of Doom*, Indy finds himself in a small village in northern India, where the sacred stones from a local shrine have been stolen. It took years for Spielberg and Lucas to iron out all the details of the story, and filming began in April 1983. Spielberg returned to the director's chair, and Harrison Ford, fast becoming one of the biggest film stars of his time, again played the role of Indy.

Spielberg did not to shoot the prequel in India because its government did not like many elements of the script. Instead, much of the shooting took place in Sri Lanka, as well as in several different sound stages on studio lots. Complications arose when Harrison Ford had to be flown by helicopter to a nearby hospital after suffering a herniated disk in his spine. This forced Spielberg to shut down production until his leading man was back on his feet. Despite these setbacks, the finished film did not go over schedule or budget.

Indiana Jones and the Temple of Doom hit theaters in May 1984 and was an instant hit, eventually earning more than ten times its production costs. Nevertheless, some moviegoers and critics did not like the story's darker, grittier tone compared to that of *Raiders of the Lost Ark*. Some shockingly graphic scenes caused the Motion Picture Association of America to consider giving the film an "R" rating, arguing that this content was too harsh for a simple "PG" rating. As a compromise, Spielberg suggested a new rating that was somewhere in between. As a result, the "PG-13" rating was born.

Something else new and exciting emerged from Spielberg's experience making *Indiana Jones and the Temple of Doom*: He fell in love. Spielberg had been previously married to actress Amy Irving from 1985 to 1989, and they had a son, Max. During the

G, PG, PG-13, R... WHAT'S IT ALL MEAN?

In the United States, the motion picture rating system was enacted to make it easy for parents to determine how appropriate a film was (or wasn't) for their children. This system was enacted in November 1968 through the Motion Picture Association of America (MPAA). Prior to this, the U.S. government had a rating board that determined whether a film was suitable for public exhibition. However, in a famous 1965 case that went all the way up to the Supreme Court, it was decided that this gave the government too much power over the creative arts— it was not the government's place to decide what the public could and could not view. It was left to the MPAA to come up with a simple rating system that would, at least, hint toward a film's content. Today, the ratings are as follows:

G – General Audiences – All Ages Admitted.
PG – Parental Guidance Suggested – Some Material May Not Be Suitable For Children.
PG-13 – Parents Strongly Cautioned – Some Material May Be Inappropriate For Children Under 13.
R – Restricted – Under 17 Requires Accompanying Parent Or Adult Guardian.
NC-17 – No One 17 And Under Admitted.

Spielberg met his future wife Kate Capshaw while working with her on the second Indiana Jones film.

filming of *Temple of Doom*, Spielberg found himself immediately drawn to actress Kate Capshaw, who played Indy's "main girl," Willie Scott, in the film. She and Spielberg dated for years after the filming of *Temple of Doom*, and were married in October of 1991.

Getting Serious

By the mid 1980s, Spielberg had clearly mastered the formula for the commercial blockbuster, and was beginning to consider doing films of a more substantial nature. As with his other successful projects, he knew this would require just the right story—and he found one in Alice Walker's Pulitzer Prize-winning novel, *The Color Purple*. It centers around a young black girl named Celie Harris,

One of the stars of Spielberg's film
adaptation of the book *The Color Purple*
was Whoopi Goldberg.

who struggles to find happiness in the American
South during the early twentieth century. Spielberg
tapped an aspiring actress and comedienne with the
unlikely name of Whoopi Goldberg to play Celie.

The film was shot in North Carolina on a budget
of just $15 million, and when it was released in
December 1985, *The Color Purple* was an immediate
commercial hit. More important to Spielberg,
however, was that both the public and the critics
embraced his first effort at making a more meaningful
film. Roger Ebert, the well-respected movie critic from
the *Chicago Sun-Times*, considered it the best film
of the year, and Janet Maslin of the *New York Times*,
while pointing out that Spielberg did alter some of
the story from Alice Walker's book, maintained that
the movie still worked very well. It was nominated for

eleven Academy Awards, although it did not win in any category.

Spielberg followed up *The Color Purple* in 1987 with another film of great depth. *Empire of the Sun* was also based on a prize-winning novel, this one from English writer J. G. Ballard. The plot centers around a young boy in Shanghai, China, during the Japanese attacks on Pearl Harbor in December 1941. After the Japanese invade Shanghai, he becomes separated from his parents and tries to survive on his own. Eventually, the boy gives himself up and is put in a camp with other prisoners. When the camp is attacked by Allied forces, the Japanese and the prisoners flee, and the boy is once again forced to fend for himself.

Spielberg directed Christian Bale in his first major film role in 1987's *Empire of the Sun.*

Spielberg at first planned to act only as *Empire of the Sun*'s producer, but after reading the novel he decided he wanted to direct it. Released in December 1987, it earned only a modest profit. However, many critics hailed it as an achievement in cinematic storytelling (although some did not appreciate the Indiana Jones-type adventure flourishes that were added to give it slightly more commercial appeal). Like *The Color Purple*, *Empire of the Sun* was nominated for several Academy Awards, but did not win any.

Back to the Blockbusters

Before the close of a most remarkable decade for Spielberg, he found himself again on one side of the camera while Harrison Ford, playing the role of Indiana Jones, was on the other. In spite of some of the negative commentary that had marred the last Indy installment, the franchise was still a global phenomenon, and the core audience wanted more. Spielberg and Lucas came up with a new adventure where Indy and his father (played by veteran actor Sean Connery) have to find the hallowed cup Jesus used at the Last Supper—otherwise known as the Holy Grail—before the Nazis do. Released in May 1989, *Indiana Jones and the Last Crusade* was made for $48 million but earned ten times that, thrilling Indy fans and acting as a kind of remedy for the disappointment of *Temple of Doom*. Spielberg was also under the impression it would be the last film in the series. At the end of the film, Indy and his three supporting characters ride off into the sunset as a metaphorical statement of completion.

One more Spielberg-directed film would be released before the decade that changed his life

For the third Indiana Jones installment, Spielberg brought in famed actor Sean Connery to play Indy's father.

came to a close. *Always* is a touching remake of the 1943 romantic drama *A Guy Named Joe*, and tells the story of an aerial firefighter named Pete who takes unnecessary chances in the air while his girlfriend, Dorinda, suffers from worry. When he finally pushes his luck too far and is killed on a firefighting mission, Pete's ghost is tasked with helping Dorinda move forward and find happiness in the wake of his passing. *Always* was a labor of love for Spielberg and its star, actor Richard Dreyfuss (they'd discussed making the film during their days on the set of *Jaws*), but it was neither a critical nor commercial success. Nevertheless, the bulk of the 1980s had been a period of phenomenal success for Spielberg, more so than most directors would enjoy in a lifetime. That did not mean, however, that he was ready to call it a wrap.

In some ways, he was just getting started.

4 MR. HOLLYWOOD

The Tireless Director

Steven Spielberg continued his reign as a reliable director of commercial hits throughout the 1990s and well into the new millennium. In 1991 he released *Hook*, the story of an adult Peter Pan. Now called Peter Banning (played by Robin Williams), he is married with a family—but has lost most of his youthful spirit. When his children are kidnapped by the evil Captain Hook, Banning goes back to Neverland to rescue them, and in the process rediscovers his "inner child." While movie critics generally disliked the film, the public felt otherwise, and it earned more than $300 million at the box office.

Two years later, Spielberg directed one of the biggest blockbusters of all time—*Jurassic Park*. Based on the novel of the same name by bestselling author Michael Crichton, it involves a group of

In spite of his past successes, Spielberg's primary interest has always been whatever movie was in front of him.

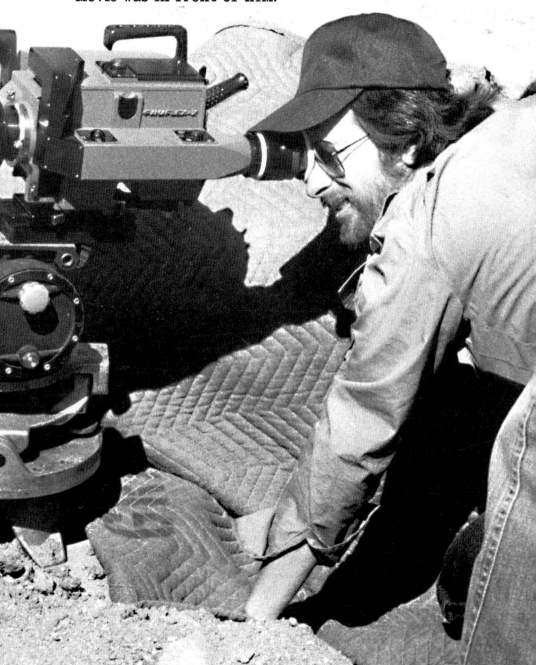

Spielberg's adaptation of Michael Crichton's bestseller *Jurassic Park* became one of the biggest blockbusters of all time.

people trapped in a wildlife park populated by on-the-loose dinosaur clones, some of whom are only too happy to include humans as part of their diet. Shot on a budget of just over $60 million and released in June of 1993, *Jurassic Park* went on to earn more than $1 billion in theaters. It was

celebrated by critics for its groundbreaking visual effects and won three Academy Awards. A few years later, Spielberg climbed into the director's chair for the *Jurassic Park* sequel, *The Lost World* (also based on the Crichton novel of the same name). Released in May 1997, *The Lost World* did not do as well as *Jurassic Park*, but was still considered a smash hit with more than $600 million in ticket sales alone.

Spielberg's lifelong interest in World War II was obvious in his production of *Saving Private Ryan.*

Spielberg had another success in 1998 with *Saving Private Ryan*, a World War II saga about a squad's search for Private James Ryan, whose other three brothers had already been killed in action. (In accordance with the military's "Sole Survivor Policy," such a solider would be discharged from service and sent home.) Featuring stars Tom Hanks and Matt Damon, the film earned a positive reception from both critics and consumers and earned nearly $500 million. On a personal level, *Saving Private Ryan* was a return to Spielberg's longtime passion for World War II stories.

Spielberg also spent some time around the turn of the century directing films that were more serious in subject matter. The first, made in 1993, and most successful of these, by far, was pulled yet again from the annals of World War II — *Schindler's List.* The film is based on the true story of Oskar Schindler, a German businessman and member of the Nazi Party who employed more than one thousand Jews in his factory as a way of saving them from the concentration camps. Twenty years later, when asked about the film in an interview, Spielberg said, "My parents, who weren't involved in the Holocaust, often talked about the Holocaust. It was a subject that was very open in my formative years, and I saw a lot of documentaries. I was just like a passive witness; I wasn't doing very much about it. I was just taking it all in...I couldn't believe that something like that could've happened in the 20th century—it was just unfathomable—but it did...When I went to Poland to start working on *Schindler's List*, I quickly realized after a couple of days of filming that this just wasn't a natural reflex of my filmmaking instincts—this was going to be something that was going to change my life." Shot entirely in black and white, *Schindler's List* has been hailed by many critics as one of the greatest films ever made. It won countless awards, including seven **Oscars**, one of which went to Spielberg for Best Director, and took in more than $300 million at the box office.

In 1997, Spielberg covered an issue of importance to the African-American community when he released *Amistad*. The historical drama is based on the 1839 mutiny by newly captured slaves from Sierra Leone who took control of the ship *La Amistad* off the coast of Cuba. It follows the international legal battle that followed their capture by U.S. maritime law enforcement officers. While *Amistad* was well-received by critics, it performed poorly at the box office by Spielberg's standards, earning back little more than its production cost. Further, *Amistad* is hampered by historical inaccuracies, thus minimizing its authoritative value.

Spielberg directed another serious film in 2005 called *Munich*. The film is a drama based on Operation Wrath of God, one of two secret attacks by the Israeli government on the Palestine Liberation Organization in retaliation for the 1972 murder of eleven members of the Israeli Olympic Team in Munich. Although *Munich* is a work of fiction, it describes many actual events and figures from the early 1970s. A riveting story, *Munich* made a modest profit, received excellent reviews, and garnered numerous awards, including five Academy Award nominations.

Producer Extraordinaire

Spielberg was either a producer or executive producer on some of the films he directed during the 1990s and into the early 2000s. He was, for example, both the director and the producer on popular hits such as *Jurassic Park*, *Schindler's List*, and *Saving Private Ryan*. However, as the years rolled on, Spielberg would often serve as the executive producer on films he believed would be successful even if he did not direct them himself.

Executive producers generally are not as involved with the day-to-day creation of a film, and in some cases they are barely involved at all. Their value often comes with the impact of their name—a film with a notable person's name associated with it will have a much greater chance of success than one that does not. In return, an executive producer can earn considerable money without necessarily doing a great amount of actual work.

The number of films, documentaries, and TV projects directed by others on which Steven

Spielberg has served as executive producer is staggering—as of the end of 2013, the Internet Movie Database (IMDb.com) lists more than 100 credited and uncredited projects—including the entire *Back to the Future* franchise, *The Flintstones*, *Casper*, *Twister*, *Men in Black I* and *II*, and the critically acclaimed *Minority Report*. He has also fallen victim to a very common trap: by becoming involved with so many projects, it is all but impossible to maintain the level of quality and success to which he had become accustomed, and some projects have not done as well.

The Mogul

In October of 1994, Spielberg took a major step toward his long-held dream of becoming the head of his own studio when he and two friends in the entertainment business formed DreamWorks Studios. He, Jeffrey Katzenberg, former chairman of Walt Disney, and David Geffen, a music industry executive who launched three record labels, each invested $33 million into the company. Another $500 million came from Paul Allen, co-founder (along with Bill Gates) of the global software company Microsoft. Within the first few years of DreamWorks' existence, several divisions were created, each with a different entertainment-based purpose. DreamWorks Records would handle musical acts, DreamWorks Interactive produced video games and other computer software, and DreamWorks Animation oversaw innovations in animation technology, to be used in movies, television, games, and so on.

In 1997, the company released its first feature film, *The Peacemaker*, and in 1998 it released its

MINOR ROLES

Early in his career, Steven Spielberg often did his own story development and screenwriting because he couldn't afford to pay others or because he wanted creative control, or both. In the 1980s—the decade that established him as a master of blockbusters—he contributed to the storylines of just two films bearing his name: *Poltergeist* and *The Goonies*. In the 1990s and the early 2000s, he helped to complete the story treatment for just one—*A.I. Artificial Intelligence*. After *A.I.*, Spielberg's involvement in the creation of storylines dwindled to almost nothing.

On another front—on-screen appearances—he went in the opposite direction. Although he thought of himself generally as a behind-the-camera person, he always enjoyed making "cameos" (a brief part in a film or television show which may or may not include dialogue). His first Hollywood cameo was as a clerk working in a county assessor's office in 1980's *The Blues Brothers*. (Steven otherwise had no involvement in this film. The director, John Landis, was a friend of his and asked him to do it.) In the 1990s and into the 2000s, he began showing up in films with increasing frequency. He played himself in both the 2002 smash hit *Austin Powers in Goldmember* and 2003's *Double Dare*, and had minor acting roles in 1997's *The Lost World* as well as 2001's *Vanilla Sky*.

Spielberg set up DreamWorks with two partners, Jeffrey Katzenberg (left) and David Geffen (right).

first computer animated comedy, *Antz*. In the years ahead, DreamWorks would, like any other movie studio, go on to produce both bombs and blockbusters. One of its biggest hits would be the *Shrek* series, whereas one of its most dismal failures, *Sinbad: Legend of the Seven Seas*, almost drove the young company into bankruptcy. DreamWorks Animation was spun off into a separate company in 2004. Today DreamWorks Studios' primary focus is film production and distribution for theaters and television, with Spielberg still involved on many levels.

Husband and Father

Although Spielberg's first marriage to actress Amy Irving did not work out, his marriage to *Indiana Jones and the Temple of Doom* co-star Kate Capshaw has. They already had four children when they were

wed in October 1991 (Capshaw had two, Jessica
and the adopted Theo; Spielberg had one, Max; and
they had one child together, Sasha). They would go
on to have two more: Sawyer and Destry, and adopt
another, Mikaela. According to the book, *Steven
Spielberg: Interview*, in the interest of maintaining a
successful marriage and a stable, happy home life,
Spielberg decided to spend less time as a director
around the turn of the century and more time as

Spielberg and Capshaw gathered with their family at an event in Park City, Utah, early in 2014.

a producer. Much of a producer's work could be conducted from home, whereas directorial duties demanded that an individual be on location virtually every day of the shooting schedule, and then in the editing room long afterward.

Still a kid at heart, Steven Spielberg would spend long weekends watching movies or playing video games with his children. It was almost as if he was playing his own version of Peter Pan.

5 TODAY AND TOMORROW

The Golden Touch Sustains

Spielberg has done less directorial work in recent years, and has been very selective about the films to which he is willing to commit his time and energy. These later releases have been quite successful.

In 2008, he released the long-awaited fourth installment in the Indiana Jones series, *Indiana Jones and the Kingdom of the Crystal Skull*. The script had been in development for years, and had undergone several rewrites before he, George Lucas, and star Harrison Ford were satisfied. Set in 1957 in the midst of the Cold War era, *Indiana Jones and the Kingdom of the Crystal Skull* focuses on an alien skull made of crystal that supposedly possesses supernatural powers. Indiana Jones attempts to get it before evil agents of the Soviet Union do. The film did suffer some criticism for storyline elements that seemed out of place in the series, but for the most

Spielberg and George Lucas returned to the world of Indiana Jones one more time in 2008 with *The Kingdom of the Crystal Skull.*

MORE INDY TO COME?

There were some new faces in the cast of *Indiana Jones and the Kingdom of the Crystal Skull*, including Shia LeBeouf in the role of Mutt Williams, Indy's son. Mutt's appearance and subsequent involvement in the unfolding adventure have led to speculation that LeBeouf may take over the franchise from Harrison Ford. Rumors persist of a fifth Indiana Jones film, with everyone from Spielberg and Lucas to Ford and LeBeouf making statements to the press hinting that it was a possibility. But, as with *Crystal Skull*, the sticking point seems to be creating a script that meets the approval of all involved. Once that's done, however, Spielberg has already expressed interest in taking up his director's duties once again.

On *Tintin*, Spielberg worked with New Zealand director Peter Jackson.

part it was another smash success for Spielberg, earning more than $750 million in theaters alone.

Another of Spielberg's recent directorial successes was *The Adventures of Tintin*, which hit theaters in December 2011. In it, a young boy named Tintin attempts to keep the whereabouts of a long-lost treasure from the main villain, the evil Sakharine. The film was based on the comics series by Belgian cartoonist Hergé, of which Spielberg was a huge fan. What made *The Adventures of Tintin* particularly interesting was that it was entirely computer animated in 3D and shot via **motion-capture technology**. This meant that much of the acting was performed by real people—including Daniel Craig, famous for his portrayal of James Bond, as well as Andy Serkis, who played Gollum in the *The Hobbit* and *The Lord of the Rings* films— but the on-screen characters were the product of computer-generated imagery (CGI). Spielberg had some assistance with production duties from Peter Jackson, the New Zealand director responsible for *The Hobbit* and *The Lord of the Rings* films. While *Tintin* was expensive to make—around $110 million—it did well in theaters, earning more than three times its cost.

Another Spielberg-directed film was released in the same month as *Tintin*. *War Horse* is about a teenage boy who develops a bond with a horse on his father's farm, then loses him to the British cavalry during World War I. In time, the boy is also pulled into the war, and they both suffer from the experience. At war's end, they are reunited and return to the farm together. *War Horse* was shot for a modest budget of less than $70 million and made about three times that in theaters. It was also hailed by critics as one of Spielberg's most powerful works and was nominated for numerous awards, including six Oscars.

The only other film Spielberg directed in recent times was, like *War Horse*, one of his most impressive. *Lincoln* describes the story of the final months in the life of Abraham Lincoln and his struggles to get the Thirteenth Amendment to the Constitution—abolishing slavery—passed through the House of Representatives at the close of the Civil War. Shot from October to December of 2011, it features some of Spielberg's finest directing (silencing critics who felt his best days were behind him) as well as a stunning portrayal of Lincoln by Daniel Day-Lewis, who won the 2011 Academy Award for Best Actor for his performance. With a budget of just $65 million, Spielberg turned the tale into an international blockbuster that earned more than a $250 million in theaters. *Lincoln* was praised by critics and movie fans and nominated for a staggering list of awards, including twelve Oscars.

Busy Executive

Steven Spielberg has continued to lend his name, time, and talents as executive producer to numerous films. Perhaps the biggest successes for him in this regard have been the *Transformers* films, including the eponymous first installment, *Transformers* (2007), *Revenge of the Fallen* (2009), *Dark of the Moon* (2011), and *Age of Extinction* (2014). Based on the popular Hasbro toy line of the same name, the *Transformers* films all have been directed by action-flick pro Michael Bay. While they have been attacked by critics for poor storytelling, weak plots, and overly simplistic characters, they have also been celebrated for their dazzling special effects and brisk pacing. They have a broad following worldwide and have earned billions of dollars, becoming one of the most profitable series in movie history.

Conversely, Spielberg's otherwise golden touch could not turn 2011's *Cowboys and Aliens* into a winner. *Cowboys and Aliens* barely covered its $165 million production budget in spite of an aggressive marketing campaign and an all-star cast that included Harrison Ford and Daniel Craig.

Looking Back ... and Ahead

Despite having a career spanning roughly half a century and a track record of staggering success, Spielberg has had his share of detractors—people who have felt it necessary to belittle his achievements. They have claimed that the bulk of his

Schindler's List had it roots in the stories Spielberg heard as a child.

work has been too shallow to be taken seriously. For every *Schindler's List*, they argue, there have been four or five lightweight films that offer little beyond escapist entertainment. Others criticize him for his films' many historical or factual inaccuracies, suggesting a willingness on Spielberg's part to sacrifice truth for popular appeal. His repeated portrayal of the "ideal American family," with its blissful suburban matrix of father-mother-children-and-the-dog has also been the target of many naysayers. Spielberg's knack for putting out films that earn galactic figures at the box office seems to infuriate many in the film industry. He has been accused of trying to monopolize the very concept of successful filmmaking and setting the bar so high that it becomes all but impossible for others to follow his lead.

Those who view Spielberg's accomplishments with such disdain are clearly the exception. Even in this age of high-tech home entertainment, where you can enjoy a story on a huge high-definition screen with surround sound right in the comfort of your living room, people still flock to theaters to enjoy the communal experience. Spielberg has done an admirable job of giving these folks their money's worth —and as he heads toward his 70th birthday in 2016 he plans to keep busy. He has said that he

Almost from the start of his career, Spielberg has been a rising star.

would like to direct a fifth *Indiana Jones* film once a solid storyline is in place, and he has committed to be the executive producer for the next installment in the Jurassic Park series as well as a second *Tintin* film.

One thing seems likely: Once people are sitting in theaters watching his movies, Steven Spielberg will probably already be working on something else.

FILMOGRAPHY

The following is a list of the theatrical releases Steven Spielberg has either written, directed, produced, or served as executive producer on as of the end of 2013. The films are listed in alphabetical order by year. For a more complete listing, including his work for television, video, and video games, please visit the Internet Movie Database website, www.IMDb.com

The Last Gun (1959 / director)
Escape to Nowhere (1961 / director, writer)
Fighter Squad (1961 / director, writer)
Firelight (1964 / director, producer, writer)
Slipstream (1967 / director, writer) (unfinished)
Amblin' (1968 / director, writer)
Duel (1971 / director)
Ace Eli and Rodger of the Skies (1973 / writer)
The Sugarland Express (1974 / director, writer)
Jaws (1975 / director)
Close Encounters of the Third Kind
   (1977 / director, writer)
1941 (1979 / director)
Used Cars (1980 / executive producer)
Continental Divide (1981 / executive producer)
Raiders of the Lost Ark (1981 / director)
E.T.: The Extra-Terrestrial (1982 / director, producer)

Poltergeist (1982 / producer, writer)
Twilight Zone: The Movie (1983 / director, producer)
Gremlins (1984 / actor, executive producer)
Indiana Jones and the Temple of Doom (1984 / director)
Back to the Future (1985 / executive producer)
Fandango (1985 / executive producer) (uncredited)
The Color Purple (1985 / director, producer)
The Goonies (1985 / writer, executive producer)
Young Sherlock Holmes (1985 / executive producer)
An American Tail (1986 / executive producer)
The Money Pit (1986 / executive producer)
*batteries not included (1987 / executive producer)
Empire of the Sun (1987 / director, producer)
Harry and the Hendersons (1987 / executive producer)
Innerspace (1987 / executive producer)
Three O'Clock High (1987 / executive producer)
  (uncredited)
The Land Before Time (1988 / executive producer)
Who Framed Roger Rabbit (1988 / executive producer)
Always (1989 / director, producer)
Back to the Future Part II (1989 / executive producer)
Dad (1989 / executive producer)
Indiana Jones and the Last Crusade (1989 / director)
Arachnophobia (1990 / executive producer)
Back to the Future Part III (1990 / executive producer)
Dreams (1990 / executive producer)
Gremlins 2: The New Batch (1990 / executive producer)
Joe Versus the Volcano (1990 / executive producer)
Roller Coaster Rabbit (1990 / executive producer)
An American Tail: Fievel Goes West (1991 / producer)
A Brief History of Time (1991 / executive producer)
  (uncredited)
Cape Fear (1991 / executive producer) (uncredited)

Hook (1991 / director)
Jurassic Park (1993 / director, producer)
Schindler's List (1993 / director, producer)
We're Back! A Dinosaur's Story
  (1993 / executive producer)
The Flintstones (1994 / executive producer)
Balto (1995 / executive producer)
Casper (1995 / executive producer)
Twister (1996 / executive producer)
Amistad (1997 / director, producer)
The Lost World: Jurassic Park (1997 / director, actor)
Men in Black (1997 / executive producer)
Deep Impact (1998 / executive producer)
Saving Private Ryan (1998 / director, producer)
The Last Days (1998 / executive producer)
The Mask of Zorro (1998 / executive producer)
The Haunting (1999 / executive producer)
    (uncredited)
Wakko's Wish (1999 / executive producer)
A.I. Artificial Intelligence
    (2001 / director, producer, writer)
Jurassic Park III (2001 / executive producer)
Shrek (2001 / executive producer) (uncredited)
Catch Me If You Can (2002 / director, producer)
Men in Black II (2002 / executive producer)
Minority Report (2002 / director)
Price for Peace (2002 / executive producer)
The Terminal (2004 / director, producer)
Memoirs of a Geisha (2005 / producer)
Munich (2005 / director, producer)
The Legend of Zorro (2005 / executive producer)
War of the Worlds (2005 / director)
Flags of Our Fathers (2006 / producer)

Letters from Iwo Jima (2006 / producer)
Monster House (2006 / executive producer)
Spell Your Name (2006 / executive producer)
Transformers (2007 / executive producer)
A Timeless Call (2008 / director)
Eagle Eye (2008 / executive producer)
Indiana Jones and the Kingdom of the Crystal Skull
    (2008 / director)
The Lovely Bones (2009 / executive producer)
Transformers: Revenge of the Fallen
    (2009 / executive producer)
Hereafter (2010 / executive producer)
True Grit (2010 / executive producer)
Cowboys & Aliens (2011 / executive producer)
Real Steel (2011 / executive producer)
Super 8 (2011 / producer)
The Adventures of Tintin (2011 / director, producer)
Transformers: Dark of the Moon (2011 / executive
    producer)
War Horse (2011 / director, producer)
Lincoln (2012 / director, producer)
Men in Black III (2012 / executive producer)
*Don't Say No Until I Finish Talking: The Story of
    Richard D. Zanuck* (2013 / executive producer)
The Hundred-Foot Journey (2014 / producer)
Transformers: Age of Extinction
    (2014 / executive producer)

GLOSSARY

Academy Award—Award of excellence given to a film and/or its cast and crew by the Academy of Motion Picture Arts and Sciences. Also commonly called an "Oscar."

anti-Semitism—Discriminating against or hating Jewish people.

box office—The area where money is collected before people go into a movie theater. It is also used to denote the total amount of money generated by ticket sales.

computer-generated imagery (CGI)—Images, both still and moving, created with the aid of computers that are then used in a movie.

director—Person who oversees the shooting of a movie.

dyslexia—A reading disorder characterized by the inability (of a varying degree) to read and recognize words and word order.

editor—Person who organizes scenes from a film after it has been shot in order to tell a coherent story.

genre—A category of artistic work, *e.g.*, comedy, drama, Western, science fiction.

Gentile—Term commonly used by Jewish people to describe anyone who is not Jewish.

Holocaust—Any great fire or other form of destruction, but also the name given to the period of "ethnic cleansing" carried out by Adolf Hitler and his Nazi Party against the Jews in Europe during the mid 20th century.

location—A place in the real world where a movie is shot, as opposed to a set created in a studio lot and then disassembled afterward.

motion-capture technology—Shooting the movements of a real actor, then turning that performance into CGI imagery.

National Film Registry—A list of films kept by the Library of Congress that are deemed to have notable value to the history and culture of America.

Oscar—Another name for an Academy Award.

producer—Person who organizes and manages a movie's production.

score—The music written for a movie.

screenwriter—Person who writes the script for a movie.

script—A multi-page document outlining the scenes, dialogue, emotions, and other details of a movie.

set—The physical area where a movie is shot.

Universal Studios—One of the oldest and largest motion picture studios in the world, founded in 1912 and located in Universal City, California.

BIBLIOGRAPHY

Friedman, Lester D. *Citizen Spielberg.* Champaign, IL: University of Illinois Press, 2006.

Friedman, Lester D. (editor). *Steven Spielberg: Interviews (Conversations with Filmmakers).* Jackson, MI: University Press of Mississippi, 2000.

Kowalski, Dean. *Steven Spielberg and Philosophy: We're Gonna Need a Bigger Book.* Lexington, KY: University Press of Kentucky, 2008.

McBride, Joseph. *Steven Spielberg, A Biography,* Second Edition. Jackson, MI: University Press of Mississippi, 2010.

Morris, Nigel. *The Cinema of Steven Spielberg: Empire of Light.* New York, NY: Wallflower Press, 2007.

Pollack, Dave. *Skywalking: The Life and Films of George Lucas.* New York, NY: Harmony Books, 1984.

Schickel, Richard. *Steven Spielberg, A Retrospective.* New York, NY: Sterling Publishing, 2012.

SOURCE NOTES

Chapter 1

Pg. 8: Bernard Weinraub, "Schindler's List: Steven Spielberg Faces the Holocaust," *New York Times*, December 12, 1993.

Pg. 9: Tina Burgess, "Steven Spielberg talks about his dyslexia: Tips, insights, and solutions," Examiner.com, September 26, 2012.

Pg. 11: Steven Spielberg, "2006 50-Year History of International Achievement Summit Master Filmmaker Address." Retrieved December 17, 2013 from http://www.achievement.org/autodoc/podcasts/artpodvid-8-spielberg

Chapter 2

Pg. 26: "College drop-out Steven Spielberg finally graduates." ChinaDaily.com, June 1, 2002.

Chapter 4

Pg. 53: Erik Hayden, "Steven Spielberg Reflects on 20th Anniversary of 'Schindler's List'." HollywoodReporter.com, February 27, 2013.

Filmography

Pgs. 68–71: "Steven Spielberg." Internet Movie Database [IMDb], retrieved December 23, 2013 from http://www.imdb.com/name/nm0000229/

FURTHER INFORMATION

Books

Edge, Laura B. *Steven Spielberg, Director of Blockbuster Films*. Berkeley Heights, NJ: Enslow, 2007.

Garza, Sarah. *Action! Making Movies*. Huntington Beach, CA: Teacher Created Materials, 2013.

Holzer, Harold. *Lincoln: How Abraham Lincoln Ended Slavery in America: A Companion Book for Young Readers to the Steven Spielberg Film*. New York, NY: HarperCollins, 2012.

Spinner, Stephanie. *Who is Steven Spielberg?* New York, NY: Penguin, 2013.

Vander Hook, Sue. *Steven Spielberg: Groundbreaking Director*. Edina, MN: Abdo, 2009.

On the Web
DreamWorks Official Home Page
www.dreamworksstudios.com/

The official website for Spielberg's production company, DreamWorks, features lots of information and media elements concerning films past, present, and future.

Internet Movie Database (IMDb) Spielberg page
www.imdb.com/name/nm0000229/

This information page about Steven Spielberg's extensive career on the most comprehensive movie-industry data site on the Web includes photos, videos, and links to other Spielberg-related pages.

Box Office Mojo / Spielberg information page
www.boxofficemojo.com/people/
chart/?id=stevenspielberg.htm

All the information you'll ever need about the sales figures of Spielberg's films, as well as which studio distributed them, release dates, and so on.

INDEX

Page numbers in **boldface** are illustrations.

ABOUT THE AUTHOR

Wil Mara is a bestselling and award-winning author of more than 150 books, many of which are educational titles for children. For more information about his work, please visit www.wilmara.com.